Dances of India

Series Editor
ALKA RAGHUVANSHI

Photographs
AVINASH PASRICHA

Mohiniyattam

Bharati Shivaji • Vijayalakshmi

Design Kamal P. Jammual

ISBN 81-86685-36-7

Published by
Wisdom Tree
C-209/1 Mayapuri, Phase-II,
New Delhi-110 064.
Tel.: 28111720, 28114437

Printed at
Print Perfect,
New Delhi-110 064.

CONTENTS

Editor's note

My first impression of Mohiniyattam or the dance of the mohini, was extremely negative. A huge, overweight, over-painted woman dancing on stage came across as the exact opposite of enticing! My instant reaction was of vibhatsa rather than shringara! Then were what seemed like repetitive movements of a rather limited repertoire. For many years it put me off the form itself.

Many years later, I was interviewing Bharati Shivaji, who also happens to be the co-author of this book, for a programme on All India Radio. She came across as a rather gentle, slightly wounded bird that was pained over the neglect of the dance form. She was dancing a few days later in Delhi and invited me for her recital.

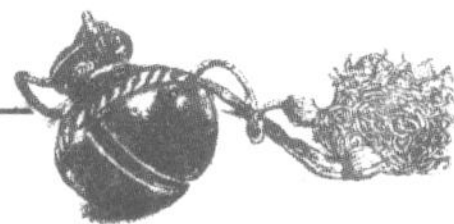

Out of sheer politeness I went. In a matter of minutes, not only did she wipe away the damage done all those years ago, but also won over a firm supporter! Despite the limitation of style, for some rasas can't just be performed in the style for the simple reason that the raison d'etre of this form is bhakti or devotion and shringara or love. Where there is love and devotion, where is the space for raudra or anger and vibhatsa or disdain?

What set Bharati's dance apart was the underlying bhakti. It was complete surrender of the dance and the dancer to the Supreme Being, which has been treated akin to the beloved by so many of our poets. Sure there was enticement or mohanam, but it was as if Radha was beckoning to Krishna. It was so ethereal and subtle that there was no question about its "otherworldliness".

The spiritual content of the form then becomes the overriding factor in deciding its quality. Spirituality that is transparent as it is palpable and the dance then becomes an offering to the Supreme Being and the dancer a mere medium. And herein is the biggest challenge of all. For dance per se is so body dependent that after a point it

becomes self-limiting. For its biggest strength - the body - is also its biggest limitation.

And Mohiniyattam, a dance devised only for mohanam, faces this major hurdle. But when the over riding emotion or bhava, is bhakti, that the strength of the dancer's training and understanding comes into play - where the spirit and thought must transcend the mere body to join the celestial in a dance of complete surrender.

Alka Raghuvanshi

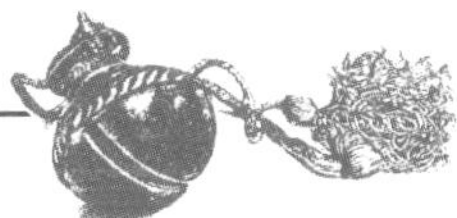

Land of the Mohini

To describe Kerala as a state situated in the southern-most part of India, along the Arabian Sea, would be putting it too simply. This narrow coastal strip with its humble, yet exotic, geographical variegations belies a culture steeped in a complex history. With the Western Ghats on one side insulating it from the rest of south India, the Arabian Sea on the other constantly exposed it to foreign influences. Today, it is an invaluable repository of innumerable art forms, because it developed the resilience to not only preserve tradition, defying several centuries, but in the wake of outside influences, welcomed them, while retaining its indigenous identity. Like Mohini, the mythological enchantress,

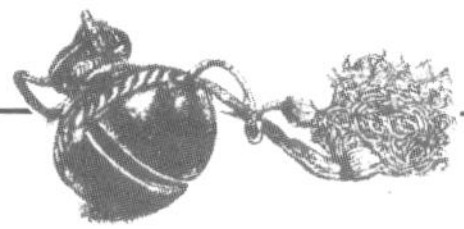

Kerala beguiled, but never really yielded. The concept of Mohini in Indian mythology is quintessentially feminine in mood, which can be classified as shringara, one of the nine rasas. The role of Mohini is exclusively to enchant, moham or enchantment being one of the noble and divine feminine qualities. Many of the Puranic legends describe Lord Vishnu, the preserver, appearing in the form of a beguiling damsel to protect the universe from evil. Vishnu transformed himself into Mohini whenever evil prevailed and righteousness had to be restored.

Feminine power is described vividly in Puranic literature. Mohini is visualised as one who is resplendent in the bloom of youth—the blossom pervading her limbs; her perfectly proportionate ears adorned with flowers; her moon-like, charming face; her rounded bosom. Her mouth replete with the sweet fragrance of the young shoots of mango; varying and confusing emotions hovering in the eyes; and her long tresses braided with jasmine. Necklaces adorn

her delicately tapering neck, bracelets jangle on her arms, anklets tinkle on her feet, a girdle encircles her prominent hips, she playfully arches her eyebrows and a bashful smile plays on her lips—such is the charm of Vishwamohini, the one epitomising ideal feminine beauty.

Indian classical dance can be broadly divided into two aspects: tandava or the masculine and lasya, the feminine. Shiva as the cosmic dancer represents tandava and his consort Parvati is the guru of lasya. Lasya literally translates into feminine grace. Adi Shankara, the philosopher-saint from Kerala, describes the divine beauty and grace of Devi while paying his encomiums to her. She is referred to as Nateswari, the queen of dancers, or the wife of Nateswara, that is Shiva. Devi is also known as Lasyapriya or one who loves feminine grace, in Adi Shankara's Lalita Sahasranama. Legend has it that lasya was taught by Parvati to Usha, the daughter of Bana, who in turn imparted it to the gopis of Dwarka, from whom

the art spread to the women of Saurashtra and later to other parts of the country. Mohiniyattam falls within this soft and graceful tradition of lasya. So divine is lasya, that Mohiniyattam could be attributed to the dance of the Devastris or celestial women.

The role of Mohini is prominent in many of the theatre forms of Kerala including Kudiyattam, Krishnattam and Kathakali, in the presentation of the Puranic legends. The transformation of a character is most significant and unique. The role of Lalita, which is synonymous with Mohini, is popularly enacted in some of the episodes of the Puranic legends in Kathakali. In Pootana Moksham, the female demon, sent by the demon Kamsa, appears in the role of Lalita, a beautiful maiden, to kill the infant Krishna.

In one of the episodes popularly enacted in Kathakali, Vishnu appears as Mohini to destroy the demon Bhasmasura. Shiva, pleased with Bhasmasura's austere penance, grants him a boon.

Bhasmasura wishes that anyone on whose head he places his hand, should perish instantly. Overcome with the greed of power, he tries to conquer the entire universe by placing his hand on Shiva's head. Terrified by his impudence, Shiva implores Vishnu to save him. Vishnu transforms himself into a bewitching woman, captivating Bhasmasura with her ravishing charm. Bhasmasura immediately wishes to marry her. Vishnu, in the guise of Mohini, agrees to marry on the condition that he accepts the challenge of an encounter in dance. As the dance culminates, Mohini assumes a posture in which her hand rests on her head. The demon imitates and is instantly reduced to ashes. In yet another episode, Vishnu appears in the form of Mohini to protect the universe from the evil demons in possession of amrita, the nectar of immortality. Where adharma or non-righteousness prevailed, Vishnu appeared as Mohini and once the mission was accomplished, he departed from this world.

The concept of the mother goddess is the most important element

in Dravidian culture. The earth deity is spiritualised as female, and it been believed that the predominance of mother-worship is a survival of the matriarchate. This enchanting land of Mohini, where salvation depends entirely on good actions, the deep remorse of matricide, perhaps, gave rise to a system in which women were to rule. The matriarchal system or Marumakkatayam, where the woman enjoyed the right to succession and inheritance, was very common among the Nairs of Kerala. Consequently, Nair women became self-reliant and unlike women from other communities, had the freedom to educate themselves.

Even regarding matrimony, a Nair woman had the right to reject her suitor. The practice of polyandry was also common, without any social stigma attached to it. According to Barbosa, 'the more loves the woman had, greater was the honour'. Shaik Zainuddin had observed that each Nair woman had more than two husbands and they seldom quarrelled. Even in the royal houses of Travancore and

Cochin, succession was nepotic. A raja was succeeded by his sister's eldest son. This privilege enjoyed by the women could have been a major force that inspired the aesthetic and cultural life, which found deep expression in many of the feminine art forms, such as Nangiar Kuthu, Kaikottikali and Mohiniyattam, to name a few.

Origin and Evolution

The earliest tradition of feminine dance in Kerala has been recorded between the 3rd and 8th century A.D. Kudiyattam performed by the Chakyars and Nangiars, is directly based on Bharata's Natya Shastra—the unique scientific and comprehensive treatise on dramaturgy. Reference to it is found in Chilapatikaram, through the term Slakyagir written around 7th century A.D., by Illango Adigal during the Chera reign in Kerala. The rendition of vachika or oral rendition was known as Slakyagir, from which the name Chakyar might have evolved. The feminine roles in Kudiyattam were performed by Nangiars, the women of the Nambiar community.

The Nangiars performed three major functions: Sitting on the stage, in full view of the audience throughout the performance, playing the cymbals to keep time for the performance of the actors/actresses and singing verses, either for invocation of gods or for vocal support to the performer enacting nirvahana or solo flashback; taking the role of women characters in the play, wearing the costume assigned to female roles in different situations; and performing the special role of Subhadra's maid Kalpalatika in the nirvahana mode in Nangiar Kuthu. It is the dramatic narration of the ntire story of Sri Krishna, impersonating the various characters in about 50 or 60 episodes without change of costume or make-up, but using the whole gamut of histrionic skills and presenting varied emotions through gestures and body language.

Nangiar Kuthu is said to have been first performed during the reign of Kulashekhara Perumal (A.D. 800). It goes to the credit of one of the ruling monarchs of the Kulashekhara dynasty that he made an

attempt to reform the Kerala stage and adopt some of the dramas that were quite popular with the audience and suited the needs of the reformed theatre. It is a unique event in the history of Indian stage where such a small group of professional actors played a singular role in preserving and propagating this great form.

Women played an active role on the stage in all dramatic performances. It goes without saying that the individual attainments of women must have been of a very high order. The small group of professional stage-actors attached to the temples certainly played a vital role in preserving the vast treasure of literature, which would have otherwise been lost to posterity.

The first play was Subhadra Dhananjayam, written and staged by Kulashekhara Perumal. The Nangiar is accompanied on the mizhavu (copper drum) and kuzhitalam (cymbal) by the Nambiars. The Nangiars enjoyed such a high status in society that they were

known as devastris or celestial women. This ancient feminine form, confined strictly to the temple precincts, cannot be said to fall completely under the lasya tradition. As in chakyar kutha, the emphasis was more on the dramatic aspect and facial expressions; footwork or charis were few, although it did comprise many charis earlier.

While Nangiar Kuthu preserved its tradition in the Kuthambalams or temple-theatres, a similar tradition which ran parallel in the Kerala temples was Dasiyattam. Most of the Indian classical dances of today owe their origin to temple dances known, as Dasiyattam. Kerala too had a temple-dance tradition which was probably introduced from Tamil Nadu.

Kalidasa, the venerated classical poet of India, mentions devadasis dancing in gay abandon in the Mahakala temple in the play, Meghdootam. Kerala was no exception in following this ancient

tradition. The Indian classical dance that we see today is partly an evolution from Dasiyattam, which flourished in the country for many centuries and subsequently, grew into various regional dance forms.

In Kerala, devadasis came to be known as tevadachi, which meant servants of God. In the early years of the devadasi tradition, dances were performed by women of royal and noble families, because the offerings were made to the Supreme Lord who demanded the obeisance of women of the highest social and cultural status. It is believed that even the Chera king, Kulashekhara Alwar, himself offered his daughter as a devadasi to the lord of the temple in Srirangam.

The attitude of the devadasis was purely devotional and their art was confined only to the temple precincts. These tevadigals were trained in the family tradition and hence came to be known as a

class, called Tevadiyar. They were maintained by the temple authorities. The earliest record of this system is found in an inscription dating back to A.D. 932 in Chokkur temple, 70 km north of Calicut, in north Kerala.

Around the 10th century A.D. when the caste system began to rise, the devadasi was assigned varying degrees of status, depending upon the conditions of her service and dedication. Some were offered to the temples by the Namboothri Brahmins, some were sold, while others received wages as dancers and musicians. Buchanan, who travelled extensively in Malabar and south Canara, has recorded that when brahmin widows became devadasis, they associated only with brahmins or with members of higher castes; the latter choice involving the payment of a separate and additional tax. The social life of these women was dignified.

Abbe Dubois, a French Jesuit and an astute observer, gives a

detailed description of the devadasis, after his association of 30 years with the people of southern India. He observes that the courtesans were the only women allowed to learn to read, sing and dance. Any other woman would be ashamed to own that she had learnt to read. Curiously enough, courtesans and dancing girls were always associated with good luck. They were supposed to avert the evil eye from the idols as well as human beings and courtesy demanded that a certain number of them accompany person of standing. To go unaccompanied almost amounted to a lack of respect.

The arati ceremony was performed for averting evil and catastrophes and was performed daily as a precautionary measure on behalf of the rajas, governors, generals and other people of authority. Whenever such personages were exposed to the dangers of the evil eye, they called on the dancing girls to perform the ceremony; some were kept solely for the purpose. Abbe Dubois

goes on to say that the devadasis were originally reserved exclusively for the enjoyment of the brahmins, but in his time they were bound by their profession to sell their favours to anybody able to pay the price. Their reputation for bringing good luck made their presence at weddings and other solemn functions highly desirable.

Dubois was surprised and at the same time fascinated by them and several times compared their quiet seduction and great taste in dress and adornment of their person with the 'disgraceful methods of the wretched beings who give themselves up to a similar profession in Europe, whose indecent behaviour, cynical impudence, obscene and filthy words of invitation are enough to make any sensible man, who is not utterly depraved, shrink from them in horror.' He adds, 'Of all the women in India, it is the courtesans, and especially those attached to the temples, who are the most decently clothed; indeed, they are particularly careful not to expose any part of the body.'

A devadasi never married; as she was wedded to the deity of the temple, she never became a widow. When a dasi died, no puja or auspicious ceremony was performed in the temple till the cremation. The deity being her husband, mourning had to be observed in the temple as well. For her initiation as a devadasi, a girl had to go through a formal and rigorous ritual. She began learning dancing and singing at the age of five. According to Chilapatikaram, the prescribed period of learning was seven years.

The talikettu ceremony or the wedding of the girl to the deity, took place at an auspicious time within the temple. A Namboothiri brahmin officiated as the high priest on behalf of the deity; he tied the tali, the sacred thread around her neck. The ceremony over, the Namboothiri imparted the Panchaksara hymn to the bride. Later, a formal induction into the art of dancing was carried out by the chief nattuvan (instructor), after which, many a time, a rigorous training followed for seven years.

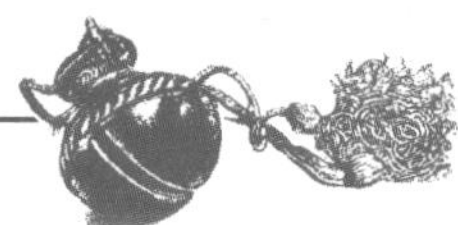

However, by the end of the 20th century, Dasiyattam reached a point of degeneration. To stem the rot, the queen of the Travancore royal family passed a law prohibiting Dasiyattam. The government decided against recruiting girls to the devadasi system, in the hope that the system would die out in due course. It is unfortunate that the tradition of Dasiyattam, a precursor to the Indian classical dances of today, with such hallowed beginnings and having been nurtured in the temples for several centuries, should have gone into gradual oblivion after continual debasement over the last few decades.

Literary Tradition

It was around the 8th century A.D., that Kerala started evolving a distinct identity of its own, separate from Tamizhagam. With the emergence of the Chera dynasty, temple architecture, script, language, philosophy and regional art forms underwent a major revival. The most prominent Chera king was perhaps Kulashekhara Alwar, the royal dramatist, who infused a new spirit into the classical Sanskrit theatre in Kerala, giving it a new lease of life, which enabled it to survive in this part of the country, while it perished in all other parts of India. The Chera period stands out most distinctively in the cultural and religious history of Kerala, marked by a great upsurge of social,

cultural and religious activities. The development of a new dialect in fact began even before the rise of the Cheras of Makotai, in the 7th and 8th centuries and came to be incorporated into epigraphy for official records in the 9th century.

Towards the close of the same century and the beginning of the 9th century came the great Adi Shankara, who produced distinguished works like Brahmasutra Bhasya, but it is for Soundarya Lahiri, his most famous work dedicated to Devi that he is well known for. The stotras or religious chants in praise of Shiva, Vishnu and Bhagavati, attributed to the great Shankaracharya are believed to have flourished during A.D. 788-820.

In A.D. 932, during the reign of Raja Goda Ravi Varma, Dasiyattam flourished, evidence of which can be found on an inscription in a Shiva temple at Chokkur. Between the 9th and the 13th century, dasiyattam was in vogue throughout south India, following more or less the same

pattern of pure devotion to gods and goddesses, and was practised mostly within the temple precincts. On the whole, the Chera period in Kerala was highly productive, as is evident from the spate of devotional songs and narrative poems, philosophical treatises, dramas, commentaries and other historical works. However, most of these works cannot be classified as great literature, except perhaps the hymns of Kulashekhara, the single drama of Shaktibhadra and the philosophical works of Shankara, the last mentioned group deserving to be treated more as products of south India than of Kerala. Creative work in Tamil appears to have ceased to come out of Kerala since the close of the 9th century and the fast development of a new Malayalam dialect, derived from standard Tamil, in this region might have been responsible for this phenomenon.

However, the appearance of independent Malayalam literary works, apart from Tolan's Vidusaka passages in Kudiyattam cannot be noticed during the Chera period. Perhaps the spoken dialect of old Malayalam,

already employed in epigraphy, came to be used in serious literature only after it attained more maturity in the course of centuries. The Chera period may truly be stated to have laid the foundation for a passionate love of Sanskrit learning and literature in Kerala, especially among the higher classes. The most significant developments in the literary field may be summed up as the production and popularisation of Sanskrit devotional songs and Sanskrit drama—the foundation of an intellectual tradition, with emphasis on philosophy, astronomy and history and the gradual adaptation of the western dialect of Tamil for use in records and literature.

There is a definite connection between the character of an art form and the social and cultural conditions under which it is born and raised. Litterateurs of the times wrote of the beauty and grace of the female dancers. An interesting observation made by Beryle de Zoete, in her book Study Of Dance in South India, describes the technique of dance performed by Madhavi in Chilapatikaram, written around 7th century

A.D. by Ilango Adigal during the reign of the Cheras. She writes:'The training of a court dancer such as Madhavi began, so that at the age of 12 she was qualified to dance before the king. It is significant that grace of form should be specially mentioned as one of the branches of art in which she must qualify; one would have thought it to be necessarily included in the art of dancing. Perhaps the distinction is between the expertise of dance technique and mastery of the art of expressive mime, or abhinaya. Her dance master is said to be an expert in Desi. Desi which actually means provincial or rural, this is of course pure speculation, but it corresponds to our own experience of cultural influence and seems fairly probable.'

Many of the kavyas and champus written from the 12th century onwards describe with poetic delight, courtesans and their social life. The courtesan was verily accomplished and was well versed in the sensuous tradition of Sanskrit love poetry. Kuttachi, meant danseuse, one who performed Kuthu, which in Tamil meant dance. Poets of that

time were great patrons of the courtesans and eulogised them in their works. The love poems were written in Manipravalam, a mellifluous combination of Malayalam of that period and Sanskrit, with the words following Sanskrit grammar and had the courtesans as heroines.

Unniyachi Charitam describes a young Gandharva, or a celestial youth, who having heard of the beautiful dancer Unniyachi, comes down to earth. A Brahmin student meets him and tells him all about her family and her incredible beauty. Gandharva spends a sleepless night, and is escorted in the morning to her mansion, where a long queue of admirers awaits him. The poem, written in Manipravalam, ends with a detailed description of the accomplished danseuse. Unnichirutevi Charitam, written in the 13th century, describes an episode in which Indra, the king of the heaven is himself attracted down to earth by the beauty of the danseuse. In Uniyati Charitam, also written in the 13th century, by Damodara Chakyar, the heroin is Uniyati, the daughter of Kerala Varma of Kayamkulam. It is a tale of apsaras or celestial dancers

where, Pravrit, while sporting in a mountain lake, captivates Chandra, the moon-god. The girl responds to his love, but the affair is disrupted by Chandra's wife Rohini, who in her chagrin curses Pravrit to be born as a mortal. Rohini later relents somewhat and consoles Pravrit that even as a mortal she would excel in music, dance and in beauty. Thus Pravrit is born as Uniyati.

Sukasandesa of Lakshmidasakavi, written around the 14th century, describes the dances performed by Rangalakshmi, a famous dancer. The heroine Uniyati is a Nangiar, and it is mentioned that Uniyati was married to the Maharaja of Cochin, and was the daughter of the Raja of Odanadu, also known as Kayamkulam. Unnineeli is described as a dancing girl, an incarnation of Urvashi, belonging to a royal family. In Kotiyaviraham, written in the 16th century, one finds some of the most romantic compositions in Manipravalam. It is really amazing how the work of an Oriya poet left such an indelible mark on the cultural ethos of Kerala.

Jayadeva's Geeta Govinda, one of the most revered works in classical Sanskrit poetry and celebrating the divine love of Radha and Krishna, was introduced in Kerala with the spread of the Bhakti movement, led by Chaitanya Mahaprabhu, in the 16th century. This gave a remarkable impetus to the Vaishnava philosophy throughout the country. In Kerala, this was a period of great creative activity.

Inspired and influenced by the Geeta Govinda, Manaveda, the Zamorin of Calicut, wrote the Krishna Geeti, Krishnattam being a visual representation of it. Like the ashtapadis, its quintessence was bhakti with shringara forming the leitmotif. Inspired by Krishnattam, the Raja of Kotarakara created Ramanattam (which later got incorporated into Kathakali), about Rama's life. The rendering of these ashtapadis has been an unbroken tradition in the temples of Kerala for several centuries. Being an integral part of the temple rituals, even today, one finds them sung in temples like the Guruvayur, in a distinctly regional style, known as sopana.

From the 12th century onwards, Malayalam, Kerala's regional language, began acquiring a distinct identity. Another very sensuous and erotic poem written in the 16th century is Chandrotsavam, meaning the moon festival. This poem, a social satire, describes the beauty of Medini-Vennilav, and other courtesans namely Unnineeli and Maralekha.

During the literary renaissance of Kerala, the erotic mood in Mohiniyattam, understandably, could have been inspired through literary sources, where the kuttachi was the subject of topical interest in society. This was the time when even the intellectually higher strata of society considered it an honour to be associated with the kuttachi. Evidence of literary works dealing with the beauty and grace of the courtesans and pursuit by the poets themselves are abundant. This was the period when, as a result of the interface between the courtesans and the poet, many a love poem were written.

The first reference to Mohiniyattam in literature, however, is to a

payment made to a Mohiniyattam dancer, in the Vyavaharamala, a work in Sanskrit by Mahisa Mangalam Narayana Namboodri, in the 16th century. We continue to find reference in another text, Gosha Yatra, by the well-known poet Kunchan Nambiar, the founder of Thullal—who lived in the court of Veera Marthanda Varma of Travancore, the predecessor of Maharaja Kartika Tirunal. Kunchan Nambiar, while mentioning the regional performing arts of Kerala, also mentions Mohiniyattam besides Kuthu, Pathakam, Pavakuthu, Thirvadirakali, etc. By then, Mohiniyattam came to be recognised as one of the most classical dance forms, so much so that in Balarama Bharatam, the monumental treatise on Natya Shastra, Maharaja Kartika Tirunal mentions Mohini Natana, among other dance forms of the desi (regional) styles.

Until recently, the state of Kerala comprised three parts: Malabar, Cochin and Travancore. Even as between these three regions, the performing arts in general were never at the same level of

development. In Cochin, the accent was more on the literary aspect, as the kings of Cochin were patrons of letters. The kings of Travancore patronised the visual arts, as they were great connoisseurs of dance and music.

A major landmark in the history of Mohiniyattam was the reign of Maharaja Swati Tirunal in the 19th century. A great connoisseur of music, Mohiniyattam received a considerable amount of royal patronage during this period. In an attempt to revive this form, the Maharaja invited the famous Tanjore Quartet, who were exiled by Sarfoji Maharaja of Tanjore and had taken refuge in Swati Tirunal's court. They were accompanied by two very accomplished Bharatanatyam dancers, one of them being a devadasi named Sugandhavalli, or Tanjavur Amma, as she later came to be known.

The present-day Mohiniyattam owes much of its structure to Swati Tirunal. In his efforts to give it a definite form, the influence of the Tanjore Quartet and Bharatanatyam seems to have played a vital

role. With his vast knowledge of the arts along with the assistance and influence of the Tanjore Quartet and dancers like Sugandhavalli, Swati Tirunal possibly enhanced whatever form of Mohiniyattam that was prevalent then. As a consequence, while Mohiniyattam was reconstructed, retaining its regional content, the Maharaja seems to have adapted the format of presentation on the stage from Bharatanatyam. As most of the original padams or songs employed earlier in Mohiniyattam had either been lost or forgotten, Swati Tirunal himself composed several compositions to enrich its musical aspect. He also persuaded Irayamman Thampi, a well-known poet and musicologist in his court to compose pieces exclusively for Mohiniyattam. Parameswara Bhagavathar, an erudite scholar of music and an excellent teacher, was employed to prescribe the mode of exposition. By then, Mohiniyattam came to be performed in the court than in the temples.

Swati Tirunal discerned that the essence of Mohiniyattam was lasya

i.e. grace, therefore the movements were so choreographed to evoke this exquisite exposition of lasya. During this time, Mohiniyattam gained popularity— it had a new face, it had charm, its music was melodious and above all, it had royal patronage.

However, the Maharaja did not live very long. His untimely demise proved to be a setback for Mohiniyattam. He died in 1847, and his successor, Maharaja Uttiram Tirunal was a fanatical supporter of Kathakali. Under these circumstances, when the royalty did not patronise Mohiniyattam, it lost all the dynamic support it enjoyed. While Kathakali was maintained by royal patrons and institutions, Mohiniyattam unfortunately, had neither. So, it declined not only due to lack of the much-needed institutional support, but also due to the fact that the spectator got more interested in the Mohini rather than the attam. Yet, there were a few dedicated artistes, who in the face of several setbacks, retained the dignity of Mohiniyattam. However, they were so few and far between that by the time poet Vallathol

established the renowned Kerala Kalamandalam, he and his colleague Mukundaraja had to scour the entire state to locate a worthy teacher. Much like every art form experiences its phases of revival and neglect, Mohiniyattam too emerged from its eclipsed state. The early years of the 20th century saw the renaissance of all the classical dance traditions of India. It was during this time that Rukmini Devi Arundale, the founder of Kalakshetra, gave Bharatanatyam its present name, changing it from Sadir.

Meanwhile, a parallel cultural revival was taking place in Kerala and in 1935, the great poet, Vallathol Narayana Menon, established Kalamandalam to revive and popularise Mohiniyattam, besides the other major art forms of Kerala, like Kudiyattam and Kathakali. Kerala owes a lot to Mahakavi Vallathol and Mukundaraja for their valiant efforts in not only locating Kalyani Amma as a teacher and Krishna Panicker as the able nattuvan, but in also persuading a few girls from good families to train in Mohiniyattam.

Technique

Of the various classical styles (vrittis) mentioned by Bharata in his Natya Shastra, Mohiniyattam comes closest to kaisiki vritti (graceful). Comprising movements, which are feminine, gentle and graceful, the Kaisiki style is most appropriate for expressing the erotic sentiment (shringara rasa). Amongst all the classical South Indian dance forms, Mohiniyattam can be singled out with admirable distinction for its distinguished characteristic body movements, marked by the graceful sway of the torso. The torso movement is at variance with Bharatanatyam and Kuchipudi forms. The ati bhanga or the

swaying movement of the torso from side to side, in Mohiniyattam needs to be explained in contrast to the tribhanga, prevalent in Odissi, another lasya oriented dance form. In ati bhanga, the undulating movements of the body create a serpentine pattern, while the technique of Odissi has the tribhanga deflection seen at three angles: The neck, hip and the knee. The swinging motion of the body (andolika) and the gentle dips in Mohiniyattam are akin to the ceaseless waves of the ocean, now surging forward, now gentle, now rising. The endless coconut trees, swaying in the soft cool breeze by the sea, could have inspired the characteristic ati bhanga movement of Mohiniyattam. The quivering of the eyebrows, so prominent in expressing shringara, is evocative of the palm leaves quivering in the gentle breeze.

The basic posture in Mohiniyattam has the feet placed two and a half inches apart, with the knees bent and turned out. Initiates into Mohiniyattam need to begin with the practice of first learning to

rotate the torso, before they are able to proceed to the actual swaying movements. This helps to loosen the upper portion of the body. This circular rotation of the torso or chuzhipu is common to the dance-drama traditions of Kerala, particularly Kathakali. It has a special significance for it relates to the generally seen circular architecture of the temples of Kerala. In fact, the circularity of the temples is distinct when compared to the rectilinear architecture of the temples of Tamil Nadu. Historically, this circular architecture might have originated from the circular mandalas or structures, so prevalent in the tantric culture, which came into prominence around the turn of the millennium.

Before the student learns the basic steps, she is made to do a series of specific exercises, with the torso movements and the foot-work, but without the hand movements. This enables the student to dance the basic steps with ease. During the course of these exercises, the student is able to experience the movements of the torso through a

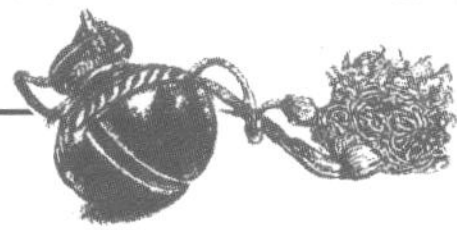

variation of foot-work. These exercises familiarise the student to the basic spirit of the dance form. The student is now introduced to the basic postures or adavus, where, the torso movement, feet and hand gestures are combined. These adavus are grouped into various sub-divisions: Beginning with the simple ones leading on to the more intricate steps. The technique in Mohiniyattam needs to be understood in terms of the essence of the dance, lasya. With shringara as the predominant mood and with grace as its motif, one can appreciate the tremendous demands made on the dancer, not just at the physical level, but in terms of the mind as well.

It would perhaps, not be far-fetched to surmise, that the technique in most of the dance-drama traditions and dance forms, particularly, Mohiniyattam, has been greatly influenced by Kalaripayattu, the ancient martial art form of Kerala. In Kalaripayattu, as in the technique of Mohiniyattam, the movements emanate from the torso, creating complex patterns, in a serpentine manner. The

emphasis is on the movement being created from the torso, while the hands only act as a pointer for the body to move.
Mohiniyattam being a quintessentially feminine dance form, the movements are extremely graceful, yet, belie an extraordinary amount of energy. Since the movements are languid and deliberate, and have to be sustained, the dancer is required to release energy gradually, as opposed to a burst of energy in a vigorous kind of movement. While the upper part of the body, waist onwards, moves languidly, it is the lower part of the body which keeps control.

There is complete absence of heavy stamping or rhythmic footwork but the steps are instead gentle, facile, soft and sliding. This is so because vigorous footwork would disturb the unique rise and fall of the body, with the emphasis on the sway of the torso. The movements are never abrupt, but dignified, spontaneous, natural, restrained and yet subtle. The vertical line of the body is never broken, thus creating a serpentine pattern in which the body sways

above the waist. A continuum is maintained, where one movement blends into the other without any sharp deflection. There are subtle moments, when two movements dissolve into each other seamlessly. And sometimes the movement unfolds even before the rhythm, to create fluidity. The glances, postures, and gait are so employed as to evoke the feminine spirit.

The chari (foot movement) in Mohiniyattam is executed with the toe touching the floor, contrary to Bharatanatyam, where the heel touches the floor. The hand movements are never angular as in Bharatanatyam, but rounded and semi-circular. Grace being the essence of the dance form, for the student to feel graceful is most essential, yet, to be graceful is a state of being which can hardly be taught, but only experienced.

The technique of Mohiniyattam is delineated with a great deal of spontaneity and ease. Its simplicity is only deceptive, for the more simple it looks, the more complex it actually is for the dancer to

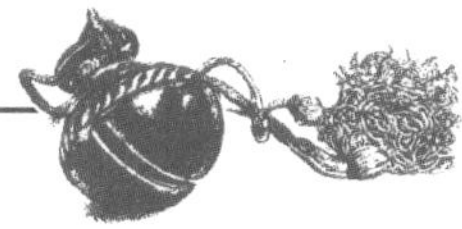

express it. It can be aptly said that Mohiniyattam has its own precision in its apparent lack of precision. Emphasis and importance are never given to mere technical perfection, for the dancer is gradually supposed to imbibe the spirit of the dance form, with swanubhava or self-experience being most necessary. What seems naturally and easily expressed is actually acquired over a long period of assimilation and experience. In Indian classical dance, the hand mudras or gestures have always been a fundamental and effective means of communication. In Kerala, it became a magical code for religious rituals, where it became a way of paying obeisance to the supreme power. In Tantra Shastra, mudras were demonstrated to please deities. It is no wonder that in classical dance, which originated from the temples, mudras form an important means of communication.

Mohiniyattam follows the Hastalakshana Deepika, a regional text for its mudras. The 24 mudras signify the 24 basic elements

required for creation or srishti tatva. Besides Mohiniyattam, all the art forms of Kerala follow the Hastalakshana Deepika, where the basic hand-gestures are single (asamyutta) and double (samyutta). Alongside these highly stylised mudras, several others came to be incorporated into Mohiniyattam in course of time and these gestures are termed as gramya or rustic. The samyutta hastas are gestures, where the mudra is formed by using both the hands. For example, a combination of both the hands could depict a lotus, Vishnu, feet, fish, crocodile, etc.

Apart from these, there are also mixed combinations called misra mudras. Both the hands are used here as well, but each hand is in a different mudra. To depict Shiva, the right is held in mrigashirsha, while the left is in hamsapaksha. Similarly, there are several things which can be suggested through varying combinations of two different mudras.

The hastas or hands are of two kinds—nritta and nritya. Nritta

hands are employed solely for pure dance, where it does not convey any specific meaning. Nritya hastas are used for abhinaya or for emoting and narrating a theme. The role of mudras is significant and unique to Indian classical dance, for every word comes to life with all its inner rhythms with the use of these hand gestures. Mohiniyattam not only has a distinct and complex technique, but its forte lies in an equally rich abhinaya. While mudras are used in an elaborate and complex manner in the dance drama traditions of Kerala, like Kudiyattam and Kathakali, in Mohiniyattam, it is not so. In Kathakali, it might take several hours to describe an episode, whereas in Mohiniyattam, the hand gestures are used in a suggestive manner to convey the bhava or emotion.

It would not be an exaggeration to say that the most stylised and complex form of abhinaya or facial expressions is found in the art forms of Kerala. Just as the body movements or the technique of all the major dance forms of Kerala were inevitably influenced by

Kalaripayattu, abhinaya practised and preserved in Kudiyattam, greatly influenced all the dance-drama traditions which evolved after Kudiyattam, like Krishnattam and Kathakali.
Mere use of hand gestures cannot completely convey emotions, unless accompanied by facial expressions. Yet, abhinaya does not only mean a combination of hand gestures and facial expressions, but has to unfold as inspired by emotions, where it becomes a complex synthesis of craft and feeling. Abhinaya in Kudiyattam and Kathakali is exaggerated, as both are essentially theatre forms, but abhinaya in Mohiniyattam is more subtle, yet intense.

The purpose of abhinaya is to create rasa in the audience. To translate rasa in one word is difficult but, loosely translated, means flavour or essence. The predominant mood prevalent in Mohiniyattam is shringara rasa which can be understood as a combination of beauty and love. For the purpose of identifying and appreciating various rasas, Bharata has codified them as follows:

RASA	MAIN BHAVA
Shringara	Rati (love)
Hasya	Hasa(mirth)
Karuna	Shoka(sorrow)
Raudra	Krodha(anger)
Veera	Utsaha(valour)
Bhayanaka	Bhaya(fear)
Beebhatsa	Juguptsa(disgust)
Adbhuta	Vismaya(astonishment)

When the sage Bharata compiled the Natya Shastra, it originally comprised eight rasas. The ninth rasa was a later addition. Its appropriate bhava or emotion is shama, or non-attachment. Although in Indian classical dance, all the nine rasas are performed, in Mohiniyattam, shringara rasa reigns supreme and permeates the entire dance form. However, the other rasas like anger, contempt, courage are also delineated, but these are all transient in nature and subordinate to shringara rasa, with which Mohiniyattam is suffused.

While discussing shringara rasa in Mohiniyattam, one cannot fail to mention the ashta rasa or eight emotions of Devi, evocatively described in Adi Shankara's Saundaryalahari. These ashta rasas mentioned in the Saundaryalahiri are ideal and most appropriate to depict the various moods in Mohiniyattam. This gentle lasya tradition derives its sustenance from Lasyeshwari, or Devi—she being the fountainhead of shringara rasa. The various moods of Devi signify the gamut of emotions experienced by the woman.

Devi is shringara personified, when she sees her Lord Shiva and is overwhelmed with love and desire; she epitomises the chastity and purity of Indian womanhood, for even the thought of another man is distasteful to her; she is envious of Ganga, who is enfolded within the matted locks of Shiva, and therefore her anger is aroused; her eyes are marked with wonder, seeing her Lord's third eye, which had been the cause of Cupid's destruction; horror grips her when she sees Shiva's body entwined with hissing serpents and her eyes

turn crimson at his valour; she is full of joy and happiness in the company of her friends and is all-compassionate towards her devotees, signifying the mother in every woman.

Shringara can be classified under two categories: Sambhoga or union and vipralambha or separation. In Indian classical dance, the theme of union and separation of the hero and heroine is remarkable for its romantic beauty, tenderness and delightful in its unrestrained frankness. In sambhoga shringara (union of lovers), the nayika or heroine, in the company of her beloved, describes the beauty of the season, the beauty of Nature and the enjoyment of play with her friends. She revels in adorning herself, decorating her chamber and indulging in playful dalliance with him in a garden. Some of the emotions experienced by the nayika in the various stages of vipralambha shringara (separation) are: Indifference, languor, fear, jealousy, fatigue, anxiety, yearning, drowsiness, sleep, dream, restlessness, awakening, illness, insanity, inactivity, fainting or even death, besides other conditions.

In Mohiniyattam, many of the padams or songs depict vipralambha shringara, where there is ample scope for the dancer to elaborate on the theme. Many of the padams describe the pangs of the lovelorn nayika, separated from her lover. This intense desire for union becomes the driving force for the padam and paradoxically lends the imaginative mind to weave fantasy, perhaps far more delightful and evocative than the ecstasy of union itself. Interestingly, in the padams composed by Swati Tirunal, the hero is none other than Lord Padmanabha. The themes mainly describe the nayika as separated from her lover Padmanabha.

In classical Indian dance, the panchabana or the five arrows of Cupid, evoke five different states of love:

1. Aravindam (lotus) creates sammohanam (mood for love).
2. Mallika (jasmine) creates unmadam (intoxication).
3. Ashokam (Jenesia ashoka) creates soshanam (paleness).

4. Chootham (mango flower) creates tapanam (heat of love).
5. Neelotpalam (blue lily) creates sthambhanam (state of Being stunned).

Kalidasa, undoubtedly the most revered classical poet of India, in his works describes the various situations and emotions of love. He describes feminine charm in a highly erotic manner. Meghadoot, by Kalidasa, is a love poem describing the pangs and longings of a hero separated from his lady love. In Shakuntalam, Dushyanta's love for Shakuntala has been woven into poetry at its most poignant. In Vikramorvashi, Pururava, the hero, when separated from Urvashi, his lady love, in a state of grief, literally goes mad in search of her.

Jayadeva's Geeta Govinda is most popularly performed in all the Indian classical dance forms. The divine love of Radha and Krishna and their union is a metaphor for the salvation of the soul itself. Jayadeva describes Krishna as the embodiment of rasas and love-incarnate.

In Lilatilakam, a love poem written in Manipravalam, the poet describes the excitement and restlessness induced in her lover by moonrise and the advent of night. The first part is addressed to the beloved while the second part is an unburdening of woes to a friend. The opening stanza describes the onset of dusk, and the messenger of Kama proclaims his intention to tease the hapless lovers, before the night is spent.

Shringara, expounded through Rati bhava, could, unless the artiste is extremely careful, cross the bounds of dignity and propriety. The hallmark of an artiste of quality is ouchitya. Ouchitya subsumes the quintessence of sophisticated culture. The aesthetics of ouchitya comprise in aptness and a high sense of propriety. Mohini in Mohiniyattam is conceived as madalasa or the one in languor. The bounds of madalasa are prescribed by the concept a of universal mother: the embodiment of love, kindness, compassion, poise and enchanting beauty.

Repertoire

The Mohiniyattam one saw on the stage some two decades ago, was confined to whatever that had been salvaged under the guidance of poet Vallathol at the Kalamandalam in the 30s, with the aid of Guru Krishna Panicker, Kalyani Amma and later, Madhavi Amma. Much of the repertoire had been lost by the time they arrived at Kalamandalam. Yet, with his determination and enthusiasm, the poet drew the maximum from them. After Madhavi Amma came Chinnamu Amma, an associate of hers, who continued the efforts. The traditional repertoire at that time comprised a Cholkettu, a couple of padams, some varnams, jatiswaram and tillanas.

These items were clearly, as is apparent by their names, influenced by Bharatanatyam, particularly during the reign of Swati Tirunal. While Cholkettu, a pure dance item literally meant the binding up of rhythmic syllables, the other items derived their names from the Carnatic music system that was prevalent in Bharatanatyam. The Cholkettu, begins with a hymn in praise of goddess Bhagavati and concludes with obeisance to Shiva, the cosmic dancer.

The jatiswaram is again a pure dance item, where there is a simple delineation of adavus or steps, set to a musical composition. The varnam also follows an uncomplicated format, where the emphasis is less on nritta or pure dance and more on abhinaya, unlike Bharatanatyam. Perhaps the most popularly performed padams in Mohiniyattam have been compositions of Swati Tirunal, describing the heroine yearning for her lover. Pandattam, or the game of ball was a later addition introduced by Mahakavi Vallathol. Owing to the inevitable influence of Bharatanatyam which crept in with the

advent of the Tanjore Quartet, the repertoire not only lacked clarity and the regional ethos of Kerala, which the other art forms had, but also remained limited and stagnant. As Mohiniyattam does not have a distinct identity of its own, a deeper look is perhaps warranted into its desi or regional ethos.

Mohiniyattam cannot be viewed in isolation, but has to be understood in its regional perspective, particularly its inter-relationship with the other traditions of Kerala, be it dance-drama, sculpturel, literature, music or any other. Elements from this rich repository of art forms have been incorporated into Mohiniyattam by interacting with senior gurus, historians, practitioners and scholars, and documenting these valuable observations. Over a period of time, the lasya underlying these dance traditions was identified, which had remained unexplored in the past. These lasya elements drawn from the other traditions, greatly enriched the spirit, content and form of Mohiniyattam, underlining those

characteristics which give it a distinct regional identity. In fact, when one observes these indigenous art forms closely, a common thread can be perceived. Yet, while all the dance traditions share a regional spirit, each form is distinct and unique. Until a few years ago, Mohiniyattam was perceived as a softer version of Bharatanatyam, or as another form of stri vesham or feminine roles enacted by men in Kathakali. However, today, after relentless years of research, reconstruction and propagation, Mohiniyattam has been established as a major classical dance form of India.

In order to expand and enhance the already existing repertoire of Mohiniyattam, items comprising invocation to Ganesha and Goddess Saraswati, as is the tradition in Kerala, have been included. Anything auspicious is always begun by seeking the blessings of Ganesha, who according to Indian mythology, is believed to be the remover of all obstacles. However, its special significance to Kerala is that there are several vaitharis or pnemonics of the percussion

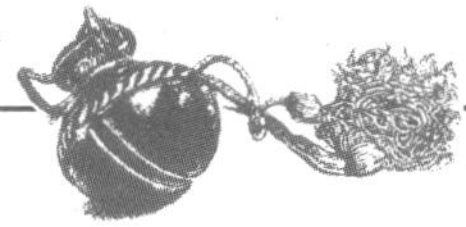

instruments, known as Ganapati talams, which are most appropriate for the Ganapati stuti. After the invocation follows the mukhachalam, a pure dance item, in which the technique of Mohiniyattam is highlighted through the graceful delineation of its characteristic movements. The dance sequence is set to some of the indigenous ragas and talas of Kerala.

Geeta Govinda is most suited to the mood of Mohiniyattam, especially the rendering of the music as sung in the sopana style in some of the temples of Kerala, particularly in Guruvayur. The Geeta Govinda being a fine blend of Bhakti bhava or the devotional element and Shingara rasa, the erotic element, the traditional sopana music only underlines the spiritual element in Mohiniyattam. The evocative sounds of the edakka, a percussion instrument, inspires the andolika or the characteristically languid movements of Mohiniyattam.

Since most of the padams in the past were confined to compositions of Swati Tirunal and limited to vipralambha shringara (separation), a breath of fresh air was badly needed, so that the other rasas or emotions could be expressed in Mohiniyattam, hitherto unexplored. Works by literary luminaries like Ezhuthachan, acknowledged to be the father of Malayalam literature and other litterateurs, like Irayamman Thampi, Kunjakutti Thangachi, Changampuzha, among others, have inspired several new choreographies in Mohiniyattam. In one such padam, written by Changampuzha, Radha is cast in the unusual mould of being past her prime. Radha and her friend are metaphoric of the metaphysical and the physical realm, the mind and the body.

A simple exchange between the two, gradually leads to a dramatic crescendo. In the beginning, the friend indulges in teasing Radha and gradually tries to convince her to forget Krishna, but towards the end, she helplessly watches Radha, oblivious to the world

around her, immersed in her passionate love for Krishna, and thinks of her as having become insane.

In yet another padam, the theme is unique and interesting. Here, there is an uncommon reversal of roles, where the nayaka or the hero is love-lorn, and not the heroine. Parvati, Shiva's consort, while adorning herself in preparation of his arrival, finds him at her door step and decides to put him through the test. She feigns fatigue and taunts him about the other woman, Ganga, ensconced in his matted locks and refuses to listen to his desperate pleas. Harassed by Cupid's arrows, he entreats her to have mercy but in the clever repartee that ensues, she tells him to go away. Finally, when Shiva confesses that he is nothing without her, Parvati relents, convinced of his love for her.

One of the other interesting padams describes the heroine confronting Cupid himself. A composition of Irayamman Thampi,

she tells him not to disturb her and make a nuisance of himself. She asks him not to exalt himself and equate himself with Krishna, who was justified in destroying Putana, the demoness.

To kindle and sustain the interest of the spectator, the repertoire has been enlivened with a wide variety of items, which are singular in their theme and presentation. For instance, there are the ballads of north Malabar, popularly known as Vadakkan Pattu, which describe the extraordinary valour of women like Unniarcha, who is well-versed in martial arts, and where there is ample scope to bring out veera rasa or the heroic spirit of the heroine.

The taratu or the lullaby, also falls within the abhinaya-oriented items, the most popular one being the composition of Irayamman Thampi, believed to have been specially written for the infant Swati Tirunal. Evocative of the beauty of Nature, the mother compares her baby with the moon and wonders who could be more beautiful.

In one of the tender moments, she mistakes the infant's cries to be the sweet song of the cuckoo. In order to balance abhinaya with pure dance, the repertoire could either culminate in Touratrika or Jeeva. Touratrika, is a pure dance item, inspired from thayambaka and panchavadyam, the percussion ensemble of Kerala. Its intricate rhythmic patterns highlight the indigenous tala system of Kerala, distinct from the Carnatic system of talas.

Jeeva could be likened to moksha in the Odissi repertoire, where the gradual increase in tempo to a crescendo, depicts the culmination of the soul with the absolute. The most poignant moment in the piece is when there is complete cessation of the song and the music, and in the silence, the dancer keeps rhythm with the sound of her bells.

The technique of Mohiniyattam is so rich and elemental, that it not only appropriately falls within the traditional frame work, but can

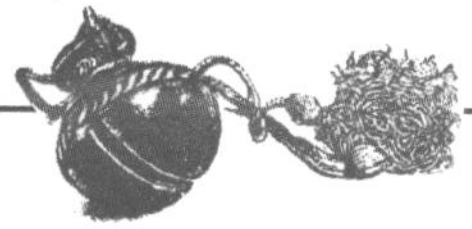

also be incorporated to enunciate more contemporary themes. Besides presenting traditional fare like episodes from the Puranic legends, mythology and other stories, the technique of Mohiniyattam has the inherent potential to lend itself to not only contemporary issues, but also abstract presentations to interpret profound thoughts.

Music and Instruments

Around the 8th century onwards, there was an upsurge of devotional sentiment and the Shaivite and Vaishnavite saints, propagated and popularised the bhakti sentiment through the medium of music. This devotional music which began developing in south India and came to be preserved in its ancient temples, came to be known as Tevaram. It does seem that sopana music is the indigenous form of devotional music, which evolved in Kerala.

The term sopana means the steps that lead to the sanctum

sanctorum, where the singer sings in close proximity of the deity. The seven steps that lead to the deity are symbolic of the seven states of consciousness and also signify the seven musical notes or the saptaswaras. As the predominant mood was devotion, the music was mellifluous and spontaneous. Sung in the temples of Kerala for several centuries, music was an offering to the deity, as part of the daily ritual.

The usage of andolitam gamakas (the swing in the musical notes) and leenam (the melting of one swara or note into another) is unique to sopana music. These gamakas are reminiscent of the andolika or sway of the torso one finds in the movements of Mohiniyattam, where, much like the notes, one movement dissolves into another.

Even today, vocal music is offered by the devotees in the temples, to the accompaniment of the edakka, known as Kottipadi Seva. It is sung to propitiate the gods and was practised only by the

ambalavasis or those residing within the temple precincts, comprising Chakyars, Marars, Poduvals, Warriers, etc. Since sopana music concentrates mainly on bhava or mood, devotion being the predominant emotion, it is also known as bhava sangeetam. The tempo is slow and the style is simple and uncomplicated, yet intense. Bereft of any abruptness or jerkiness in the rendering, this unaffected form of music epitomises the deepest of emotions and is meditative not only to the singer, but the listener as well. Sopana music is so distinct from Carnatic music, that the same raga could sound completely different when rendered in both the styles. It is interesting to note that, the same raga could be employed to express contrasting emotions, in different situations by stressing on particular notes, as in Kathakali.

Forms like Krishnattam, Kathakali and Ashtapadiattam were danced to the accompaniment of sopana music. Some of the ragas sung particularly in sopana music are Samandamalahari, Padi, Poraneeru, Indalam, Khandaram and Desakshi. The tala system in

Kerala, like the system of music, is completely at variance with the other south Indian disciplines. The talas are distinctly regional. One of the most distinguishing aspects of the talas is that the progression in rhythm is not linear, as in Carnatic music, but is gradual, as is most conspicuous in the traditional percussion ensembles, known as panchavadyam and thayambaka. The tempo gradually builds-up to a crescendo, depicting the intensification of both the spiritual and aesthetic experience, which is the essence of sopana. The talas commonly employed in Kerala are very different from those found in Carnatic music. This rich variation in the tala patterns exists in almost all the dance traditions prevalent in Kerala, such as Kudiyattam and Kathakali.

The main percussion instrument used in Mohiniyattam is the edakka. Made of jack-wood, with the tender inner layer of calf skin stretched across a circular ring placed against the mouth of the drum on either side, it is perhaps the only percussion instrument on which musical notes can be produced. It is a unique percussion i

nstrument as it can produce both rhythm and melody simultaneously, thus providing a rhythmic and melodious accompaniment to Mohiniyattam. The other musical instruments used in Mohiniyattam are the mridangam, veena, flute and the cymbals.

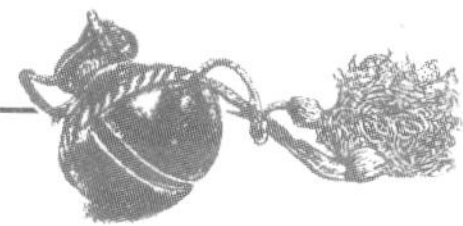

Make up & Jewellery

In Indian classical dance, abhinaya can also be expressed through costume, jewellery, make-up and other adornments, collectively known as aharya abhinaya. In Dasiyattam, the dancer was considered wedded to the lord and hence, adorned herself in all her bridal finery. The Kerala bride also wears the mundu veshti or the traditional two-piece saree which is white, bordered with gold.

The traditional costume worn in Mohiniyattam is white with a gold border, called kasavu, which has a satvik appeal. In many of the rituals and religious ceremonies in Kerala and indeed in the

day-to-day wear of the people of Kerala, one often finds white being worn extensively. The white costume with a gold border exudes an ethereal as well as alluring charm, the white symbolic of purity, positive approach and beauty. Appropriately, white is the varnaraja, or the king of all colours. Saraswati, the muse of learning, is often portrayed as attired in white. Above all, the white costume does not distract the rasika or spectator from experiencing the pristine beauty and grace of the ati bhanga movement, which could be mitigated by using flashy colours. The costume comprises several pleats, so that every time circular patterns are made, it imparts tremendous grace to the dancer and accentuates the essential spirit of the dance form.

The jewellery of Kerala makes for a most interesting study not just in terms of aesthetic pleasure but also helps the elucidation of ancient culture. Prof. Ridgeway could not be more apt when he said that the ornaments in Kerala owe their origin mainly to magic and

less to the love of adornment and decoration. Endowed with physical beauty and surrounded by a rich and bountiful Nature, the ancient people of Kerala paid little attention to outward embellishment, either in dress or jewellery. With advancing civilisation changes have been introduced, but the earliest ornaments of Kerala have a ritualistic bearing. It is significant to note that it was not the custom in Kerala to wear ornaments on the crest of the head, the nose and the upper portion of the ears.

A study of Kerala jewellery reveals certain beliefs that have been held since ancient times. For instance, it was believed that everyone must wear a bit of gold on account of physiological reasons. Those who could not afford gold wore silver, seeds, nuts and stalks of certain seeds, particularly the seed of elanji and also nails, claws, teeth and hair of animals, especially the claws of tigers. The teeth and hair of elephants were also used as amulets and ornaments, as they were supposed to act as charms.

This fact is borne out by the existence even now of the palakkai, made of the seed of the pala tree and the pulinakha mothiram, that is the ring, made with the claws of a tiger. The former is worn in the belief that it will secure the benign influence of Bhagavati (the patron goddess of the Malayalis) whose favourite is pala, while the latter is supposed to be a cure for nightmares. In another ornament, called the tali, worn by the women, the conventionalised representation of Bhagavati was originally the symbol.

Later, it was modelled like the hood of a serpent or shaped like a full-blown lotus. But the ornament, which is most connected with magic and ritual, is the yentram kulal, garland of yentrams (symbols), in which a copper leaf is impressed with mystic symbols to protect the wearer from evil spirits. These early ornaments show traces of animal worship, Nature worship and image worship. Jewellery in Kerala is in sharp contrast to the traditional jewellery of

Tamil Nadu and is very distinct. While the temple jewellery of Tamil Nadu predominantly comprises red and white stones, a significant motif which figures in most of the ornaments in Kerala is the naga or the serpent. The popularity of serpent worship could be the reason for this. The ornaments worn by the Mohiniyattam dancer are made of gold. Gold is a symbol of the sun, light, purity, truth and immortality, which can be attributed to the dance of the Devakanyas, or the heavenly damsels. The dancer wears a large pair of round ear-rings, known as toda, and the necklace comprises the traditional nagapadam, in the shape of a snake-hood, and the elakatali, a necklace with shimmering leaves of gold. The bangles as well as the waist-belt are made of gold. The Mohiniyattam dancer wears bells made of brass, just as in the other classical dance forms of India.

Perhaps in no other country has so much imagination and artistic thought been applied to the art of hair dressing as in India. The hair-

styles were inspired by the social and geographical necessities, as much as by the aesthetic consciousness of the people. The coiffure of Mohiniyattam is distinct from the other classical dance forms, where the hair is generally plaited or tied into a knot, at the back of the head. In Mohiniyattam, the hair is gathered on the left side of the head into a bun on top. In many of the temples in Kerala, one finds sculptures with the similar hairdo as in Mohiniyattam.

In ancient times, women in Kerala washed their hair thrice a day, as part of the daily routine for religious reasons. Abundance of water throughout the year in rain-fed Kerala had a pronounced influence on the local people's penchant for cleanliness. Even today, it is by no means an uncommon sight to see a cluster of women washing their hair in their characteristic way in the placid waters of the rivers, rivulets, ponds, sleepy lagoons and the languid backwaters. Their hair used to be gathered on top, only to be washed again at noon and in the evening. Perhaps, in course of time, it became a

pronounced feature of their daily life and constituted an integral part of the cultural life of the womenfolk.

Some of the old paintings are seen with members of the royal family, in the traditional hairdo. Eventually, the hairdo became associated with the classical dance style of Mohiniyattam. This, more than anything else, singularly distinguishes it from the other Indian classical dance forms, lending it an exotic grace and appeal. Interestingly, in Dasiyattam, the hair used to be plaited at the back, but gradually the hairdo shifted to the top. A string of jasmine tied around the bun only enhances its beguiling beauty.

The cult of serpent worship prevailed in Kerala since ancient times and the nayanmar was often identified with naganmar, who believed in the worship of the serpent. The top knot of the nayar is symbolic of the serpent's hood and the serpents were regarded as elements of immortality.

Picture Captions